WOMB-WEARY

ALSO BY JAMES RAGAN

Poetry
In the Talking Hours
Womb-Weary

Plays
Saints
The Gandy Dancers
Commedia

Translations
The Collected Poems of Yevgeny Yevtushenko
    (Edited with Albert C. Todd)

WOMB-WEARY

Poems
By
JAMES RAGAN

To Taelen,
for the magic of your soul
in all the voices you share,
Best Wishes,
James Ragan
8-28-08

A Birch Lane Press Book
PUBLISHED BY CAROL PUBLISHING GROUP
New York

A Birch Lane Press Book. Published by Carol Publishing Group. Editorial Offices, 600 Madison Avenue, New York, NY 10022. Sales & Distribution Offices, 120 Enterprise Avenue, Secaucus, NJ 07094. In Canada: Musson Book Company, A division of General Publishing Co. Limited, Don Mills, Ontario. All rights reserved. No part of this book may be reproduced in any form, except by a newspaper or magazine reviewer who wishes to quote brief passages in connection with a review. Queries regarding rights and permissions should be addressed to: Carol Publishing Group, 600 Madison Avenue, New York, NY 10022. Manufactured in the United States of America.

Grateful acknowledgment is extended to the following publications in which these poems originally appeared:

Antioch Review: "Out of Context"

Bellingham Review: "The Birthing House of the Blind"

Colorado Review: "To the Boily Blind Boy the Sun Spins," "Waking to Two Moons"

Crosscurrents: "Third Grade Sister of Charity"

Denver Quarterly: "Breath," "The Painting of the Steelworks on the Old Bank Ceiling"

Indiana Review: "The River in the Tree"

Minetta Review: "Fires Across the River Grande"

Missouri Review: "Birthing the Stillborn"

New Letters: "A Killing in the Old Country," "The Lake Isle of Bled"

North American Review: "The Falling Accidental"

Ohio Review: "Once the Prehistoric Man"

Southern California Anthology: "Junkman," "Understanding Mortality on Cascade Ridge," "Child Christ at the Top of the Stairs," "The Exploration of Space for the Twentieth Century Poet," "Monongahela," "The Tent People of Beverly Hills," "Motherskin," "A Boy Falls Into Space at the Stone Quarry," "Exorcising the Lane," "The Rivers of Paris," "The Debris Stone"

The Windsor Review: "Memorial to a Cow Slaughtered at the Height of Depression"

Yankee: "The Astronaut"

With appreciation to:

The Fulbright Commission

The MacDowell Colony

Library of Congress Cataloging-in-Publication Data

Ragan, James, 1944–
    Womb-weary : poems / by James Ragan.
    p. cm.
    "A Birch Lane Press book."
    ISBN 1-55972-053-0 (hard) : $14.95.—ISBN 1-55972-057-3 (pbk.) : $8.95
    I. Title.
    PS3568.A39W66   1990   90-2274
    811'.54—dc20   CIP

For Debora

Of whose Merlinian whims
of childbirthing—
Tera Vale *and* Mara Jamé—
I can never be weary

CONTENTS

III WOMB-WEARY

Womb? Weary?
He rests. He has Travelled.

—JAMES JOYCE
Ulysses

WOMB-WEARY

THE RIVERS OF PARIS

"breast-deep in descended bone."
—DYLAN THOMAS

It is raining and the boulevards of Paris
are breast-deep in bones. It is usual
for images in the rain-lay of April
to merge like ascending elms
down Saint Germain or Saint Michel.
The boulevards are the rivers wind owes
to the eyes' reflections, light
to the panes transparent
in the domes of air wind weaves
along Sacre Coeur, the sphered
mirrors in the belly-up
of imitation louvred upon the water
the lone gull skims, antiqued
in its art of flying.

Down the Seine all troves
of antiquity have bones,
the fluid and the permanent,
the rock, the sea's seed,
the hunk of air
swinging between two trees
along the banks of Quai Voltaire,
the wheeze of wind
in the *clochard's* lung,
shelled and fractured
by screams in the night air.

The bones of leaves along Pont Neuf seethe
when spearing the unpredictable
sheers of grass growth.

3

The bones of Baudelaire
have bones, timeless weights,
looms of ochre in their bethel's shapes,
poem-shadows like Norse runes
or punctuations, splintered
by the bones of spiders'
writer's tongues.

In all our streams of consciousness,
the rivers of Paris run
down the escarpments of imagined time,
their portmanteau of images
falling, boned together
like language or bat wings
aspiring to inspired flight.

In the single dying of a stone's
last breath there is progress
we will all come to
in time, falling, each of us,
through the rain of our breath,
imitations of the Dantesque,
fused by the body's currents
down the chutes of Montparnasse,
birth-wet and river-deep
in bones descending.

I

The Birthing House

While the rain of your fingertips falls,
while the rain of your bones falls,
and your laughter and marrow fall down,
you come flying

—PABLO NERUDA

THE FALLING ACCIDENTAL

Always when I think of the other-born
and the accidental falling
twins from the world
hanging on a hinge
to delicious space, cool
as the icebox I spoon
for a dish of vanilla,

I feel the age of rain
each morning the body brothers
gone, trading air for their sleep,
awaken my mother's voice
in bed, craving breath.
It is always the same. Everywhere
the odor of vinegar and stale madeleine,
everywhere the month's failed fluid
splits its sack and calmly

it is noon on Halloween and I know
the falling accidental
loss of memory
when the tongue dishing out a nut
cracks a tooth and the imaginary
axe falls, splitting
the whole breath of my lung.

Always when I think of the other-born,
the war world wanes
in its pity of the unified grave
outside Krakow, Lidice,
or the nunnery pits on Salvador's road.
Old grief passes
as if on All Saint's Day we cohabit

the same anguished comprehension,
as if by instinct the limbs
memorize their body's
history of loss. Always when I think

of the other-born, I eat
ice cream, and each accidental falling
child come-apart
remembers how the nerve buzzed first
from the rind to the core, how
in the age of separation
the terror seeps through,
cold and god-lost, cracking
the last significant bone
in our generation's thought.

BIRTHING THE STILLBORN

The year will pass so slowly
you could wade the bathtub length
long enough to boulder the moss,
the blood shute gleaming
on the round of your knees. You kneel
in the same salt bath father draws
for the weight of their bodies, forgiving.

You have in mind the neighbor
leaning strap-thin against the rain spout
warning you of dangers to the rain.
In your mind the world grows just the same
and the body of the cow
she threatens to burn is God.
She is screaming at all foreigners
who foul the free space of her ground.
You are Slovak and eight months bound
by the rope you steer around your belly
to suspend your sons in space
and keep their souls from falling.

Someone has opened the kitchen door,
let in the soul of another,
faceless as a thin weed. It is your neighbor,
spreading the long wire of her arm
like a clothesline around your body.
She would hang your sons, one by one,
by the knots of their breasts. You can feel
in the dark oblivion womb
the lynch kick of their knees each time
she leads the roped cow further
down the yard to authorities.
This is what you will always remember
about their birth, alone and forgiving.

9

MONONGAHELA

1

When we walked its broad shoulder,
Shawnee *river of hills,*
where once we did not know
to swim, or how
we cursed in our hearts
to go swinging out across its neck
in inner-tubes, our legs pushing through
their fetus force of life,
we did not know we crossed
the body of our father
above and back, and into
the weir of our birth.

In India we name the river *Ganga,*
the anointed locks of hair
through which water flows
and where on slats of sandalwood
the pilgrims wade to find the source of light.
In Pittsburgh years ago at the point
where the rivers meet
I felt the need to dip deep above my head
as if some power urged
like Shiva to resist
the dark mind-water of the swells
and search for the heart in all things drowned.

Past the launder and the bridges, past
the barge shed, welled up with spines of lizards,
past the pilings of old lucky-stones
I skimmed across the water
when the water needed fed,
I dove bathed by lobes of blood-root

10

I did not know to quench
or when, in stride, to feed my clothes.
And darting through the swash, aimlessly
like a minnow begetting itself to forget itself,
I settled in this font to sleep
in the incense of my father's bones,
the forty years of smoldering culm and mill ash
I stoke close to my side
remembering. And remembering.

2

Once when I imagined
I could sleep so sound the steep
prows of minatory boats
seamed their Saturn course of stars,
I heard my mother calling from the sky tucked away
in the sun corner of the shoal.
Free in the half-dark
and floating-fall of child's air
I passed beneath her arms
in slow swing-songs of light;
"I baptize Jame," she said,
"in the name of our daughters, sons,
and holy night."

Into the magic font of night stars,
I go with the children
to the Ferris wheel at Kennywood,
through the river's fancy dark passing
down the tunnel's sluice
where the black laughing lady quakes
and steam from the lion's mouth at Noah's Ark
loops the wind through cuddle skirts
and shirt-tail flumes. And I climb

11

the pirouette of light, up beyond
the water crest and vertigo of downward glide,
the calliope's midnight song,
where like the Pippin, poised
in its stalled race through vertebrae of wind,
all the fear sucked out and in,
I ride the heart's stone down
into the water's deep mind.

And I remember to awake,
revived by the weight of my mother's hair
still above me, flowing Monongahela,
holy water of the steelyard moon
in whose locks I drown
as in the tress of golden hair, wet
and waist-long in their eighty years,
I watch my mother comb eternally.
In full view of my father she shakes her hair dry
like an aspergill blessing the earth
and in return to be blessed.
In her prayer of a daily brushstroke,
the slow passion for living still
crawls like shade through water light.

THIRD GRADE SISTER OF CHARITY

Sister Amadeus chalked the sky of a circle
and showed us how the soul is always white.
We looked at the slate. She showed us how

in this coal-dark universe I counted badly,
one, two, three, seven, and gypped her
change for a Coke bottle. Always

in her white circles, I lost my soul.
She told us how each time
she blacked out the sky with the eraser head

I had sinned mortally, that an all black soul
is damned to emptiness. And I knew it.
So the next day at recess playing tag

I mimed my damnation. Eyeballs dilated,
sins staring through the pupils, I scatted about
in circles, scared like the devil to be *it*.

for H.M.

CHILD CHRIST AT THE TOP OF THE STAIRS

How the rain-day froze
the dark walk stair, the ceiling bulb,
the child's avenue of stars,
and the body wood from Infant Prague,

so often to its eye I knelt,
my brother in pajama tops,
the figure of a seal slapping up the palms
to the soddy thorn of its sacred heart.

It was always the same—moonfall, eglantine,
my mother at the head of prayers
I memorized like alphabets in school.
Across the hall, musk-scent, my father's

unstrung beads like a rosary
on the sole of his iron mill shoe,
the skin tongued out, leather
rasping the bed's vestibule.

Nightly to the wood I prayed
for a sign, some miracle, the slightest twitch
on the tincture lip. And just as quick
it shivered, at first the toe, slow-motion,

then the foot, in tapping time and swift gyrations,
it tapdanced wildly down the stair,
somersaulted, kicked the wall like Fred Astaire
and pranced the ceiling. I was in awe

of dancing wood, shapes of metaphor
suggesting idea, and prayer, the dancing shoe

of imagination. I was poet of the body rood,
the Bernadette of Lourdes, praying

for the dark to speak, for the long
shoe tap to the clap of the holy beat.
Each night I danced to words and rimed my feet.
God was soul and alliteration. In the name

of my father, son, and the hollow ghost,
lead me finally into Hollywood
and into temptation—and into that poetry
we were always praying.

MEMORIAL TO A COW SLAUGHTERED AT THE HEIGHT OF DEPRESSION

1

On a bench in the dark cellar
where my father's iron file

smells of grease and old pine
and rows of nails in half-penny

lay beneath the shavings
of cut skin and two-by-fours,

a rusted sledgehammer
shadows the wall guiltily,

its chipped nose and aim defiled
like some war icon to Viet Nam.

My mother says to leave it be
and dreams she sees the same cow's

head fall beneath its thunderous clap,
the deep knee-bend, the flank's

obscene genuflection, and hears
the sudden slap of eyes

lifting prayers to the moon
of father's strong arm

and says to leave it be;
there's sorrow in its breath.

2

In those early days of neighborhood, a cow
kill came slowly, a last resort

in drought when the final teat gave out
its sour dose, and milk was stored

preciously in ice-cold cellar floors.
Father dug the cow's great grave pit

there beneath my brother's Ford, the spilled
grease dripping down from its belly

through the wood ties along the cured
shanks and salt packs. My mother says

in bad times it's hard to tell
the blood stains from the oil and remembers

how when she buried the cow heart monumentally
like a lunch tomato in a knapsack,

she heard my father moaning through the window
like some fixed cat regretting loss

and remembers how she blessed herself
for all our lives and says

in bad times it's hard to tell
how we could survive, otherwise.

THE RIVER IN THE TREE

In the hollow where the dark spits up
cat's teeth in white and cheshire green,
I hear the wind click down along the willow spars
like crackling leaves in chimney fire,
and know the river in the tree.

It is May always and the same willow
sprays its haunt of lilacs down the watercourse.
All month the dozers sweep the hillside up
and toss it down in puddles. It is said
the stream is swamp and old for rooting.

In sleep I hear its false voice calling
like the dance of air when the crickets sing.
All night the swish slag pours into my ear,
and sparks of evergreen and potato pokes
drip in mud pouched like melting butter.

Above the iris path I hear the quiet passing
of the swing rope slicked by finger oil.
With bony child's feet I served the sky
and leaped for the greater good
to the solid slag of the city side.

I know the past needs leaving like the river
my body makes to root all grounding leaves.
Today my neighbor tilts his finger to the air,
and praising axe handles, fells the windless willow.
It lies old for rotting, the good for nothing.

EXORCISING THE LANE

Each autumn when we walked the dirt barefoot
and memorized the lane's long language
in the dead breath of leaves,
we heard the stone's hard breathing
beneath the late snow of October,
the sun-grunt in the moss shoal of its stomach,
the fast fall of dust feeding our brains.
When we rode the sky to pasture
high on the cow's peak in March,
my brothers limping shank to thighs
in mud bottled up to their knees,
we heard the gurgling ground swallow
of small shoe leavings, the lost believings
our world war sons prayed
incarnate like fate or wood attached to legs.
In all our minds our lives were made up
of the lane's earth birthing. Mother
heard its low death-breath across the rug
she'd broom-beat in the winds of June,
in nest seeds threshed from the rain spout,
in soot from the scopes of our outdoor cups.
Each spring she'd pray for cleansing
the rain rust from our tongues. Always
the lane coursing its breath to our throats,
and always our mother beating it back, dust-swollen,
standing her own dark ground.

THE PAINTING OF THE STEELWORKS
ON THE OLD BANK CEILING

Like death, its train stalls
in the center of future. It is nowhere
fast, but its miner
stands, always, at the train gate,
pick and gear, head to sky,
and flexes in the amber sun.
The soot is moon-yellow
and the truck tops reddish-brown.
In his eyes there is always
a reflection of fleshed clouds, a spire,
a pink bride's-thigh
and billowing breasts
across the street we never see.
There are no black leaf trees
or spudded roots and rented gutters,
no old bones to run to.
The artist gives away nothing.
Streets are never barren
in such pastels.

for RH

JUNKMAN

a.

Saturdays when the laurel swayed east
across the sun shade of the bedroom
and the odor of ditch-dirt and kerosene
swilled in the air on closet hooks,

his truck bell tolled so wildly the window shook
the belly of the sky and the familiar
call of the forager rose like a hawk
off some sleek cliff in our prehistoric hearts.

We'd shout clothes on down the stairs and out
across the slag of Hudson slope.
The grass grew niggardly. Pig iron
swooned all scavengers to greed

and rocks the rain exhumed released the ore
and skeletons of our found lives.
Fathers we became, husbands, unyielding,
kin to jackhammer and ox.

b.

In the children's ghetto where the junkman bends
infants close to the ground, listening
like stones to the low rumble of the earth's division,
we scooped up bones of shale for the diviner

who sometimes, when he'd pick us up
to tip the scales, would find in spuds of sod
a handprint, fossiled, brown and brittle.
And we'd imagine fathers turned steel, their body ruins.

We would not settle for the promised toss
of a dime or nickel, nor the future.
We offered shards of our flesh to his divining rod
to learn, by touch, in the skin of metal

the rare caress of a woman's thigh.
In our shanty lives we adored his altar to the world,
girls, truck-full, with stippled spoons on brassy beds
and imagined God in the round skies of their breasts.

In the mills, old as the earth, we grew indifferent
and worshipped cosmically like atavistic apes.
Fire, the born actor of life,
danced and smoldered in our limbs.

Each night we lay on wives and dreamed
of nipple pipes and belly stoves, and hard slab steel,
for whose adulterous touch our passions soared.
We traded souls to Mephisto,

junkman of the breath's winged stone,
to watch in the gentle alchemy of a Sunday priest,
the perfect sleight of hand—
changing wine to blood, slag to iron.

MOTHERSKIN

to a Slovak mother

Born of wheat root and summer rusk,
born of rain, sheened gold as hair swirled
in the soft comb you rake and truss,
you delight in a mirror or a photograph
or the touch of any son. When you bale

bread one by one with prayer hands,
the heart of hair on every child's arm lingers.
You blush at a wedding dance
and love counting fingers

when I play the boy and promise to die young.
All day in the shadow wood of the green martyr,
you kneel, your *babushka* slung
high across your shoulders. You can never die.
The earth would cease to grow and only know water.

The shale beneath the house has claimed your hair
possessively, the way spring water fawns moss
for breath or the wash of fresh air,
the way childskin seeks a bed to smoothly lie across.

THE BIRTHING HOUSE OF THE BLIND

From behind the stray day dog
a green wist of light curls
across the floorboard and for a moment
the sun smokes between the garbage pail and stair.
Down the hall chicken bones
branch the firmament of tile and tin;
a lone boy swings in air,
thoughts rinsed by mind wind.
He has saved the day for nothing.

He has saved the day for stones
and panes of sky the body father
cleans to blind his healing eye.
And when the midwife heaves the wailing clap
in space a hundred drums deep,
he is a boy the moment's sun
no longer keeps alone and curious.
He would rather not. He would rather
not hear the silence wake
the neighborings of the universe,
the bones of it colliding,
stray as dogs, tin on litter.

He wants to run the day from birth
to where the first light nesting
births the moon and stars,
and stones are suns
that glitter in the human skull.
He will trust no human kind
of gesture, no touch or blinking eye
the dark remembers, no passion,
no body world recalled.

II

The World Room

. . . in which each mostly wanders alone
and in this familiar-strange room.

—*GALWAY KINNELL*

THE TENT PEOPLE OF BEVERLY HILLS

Faceless on the Boulevard of Mirrors,
north along the flats of Rodeo Drive's
stripped bald head mannequins,
they come treading on
the fears of high fashion,
tents on their backs
and on their cheeks the beach
black tar of tasteless chic.

    As if to dress were not enough,
    we would have them wash
    our backhand slap
    from their Rimbaud faces.

And all through the supple stick lash
wands of their eyes, all
through the wind whiskers
of fishbone and sour cream
curdled by fame,
they see along the fruit stalls and deli box bins
of Wilshire Boulevard,

the world in the room
of their small walk-space;
they are never certain
whether they are merely asked
to fill a role like memory
in a thoughtful dream of place
or live always short of major
in a dying minor sort of way.

As if to live were time enough.
We would have them end
beyond their means.

Hours long they scrabble
onto walls and mirrors
the words they would like to leave us,
the haunted prints of thought-falls
drifting out of mind's possession
like nostalgia or grief.
The world has lost its face.

There are no hobo kings or pioneers
late to live by. When they lie
above the windy steam of sewer grates,
dream-still and all-mind gone,
they warm their body holes to sleep.
They wake to be awake.
In the dreams of many
who never took the road
to gypsy sorrow, breathing is enough.

   It is a mistake to feel themselves alone,
   to fill their skyholes up with dark.

There has never been a need
for crying, the dying say.
Once we move within the final
inch of breath, there is no other.
There are a million tents in the universe
with holes we mistake for stars.

UNDERSTANDING MORTALITY ON CASCADE RIDGE, LAKE TAHOE

Off this road one mile high in the ice
of late winter, the deer and all boned creatures
belly down into the lake's thin air.
Their tall lean noses, skating beneath
the rocks of their dawn-brown eyes,
cut a trail along the sluit.
The fawns have slept through April.

Miles above and snow-heavy,
our Caddy lacs along in fog drift.
The inch of road still hanging
like a gib between two clouds
swings to avoid our tires. And we prowl,
tight-wired, up along the sleek cliff's crown
to a rock ledge of flurries. Blinded

below the miles of failed timber,
a lone bear shakes free
the quarry of fur he prepares to bury.
Beneath the boneyard's sleet, he forages
the hunter's ground for sleep.
He has confused our snow
with the dusk of November.

We would photograph his sleepwalk
for our children, unborn, uncertain
as to any hope of their arriving.
No one grows, impatient. Nor less mortal.
More and more as he guts the bark's deep bed
for a bite of darkness, the bear remains
content with his insomnia, we with driving.

FIRES ACROSS THE RIVER GRANDE

Yesterday five inches of snow
fell where the huts grow along the slopes.
Today, five fires light the children
living nearby, huddled in place.
It is November and the sand
needs burning like bushels of grass.

When the fire pits dim,
the children sink their hard knees
into the ash. The sand warms their buttocks
like a hot door of an oven. This season
their bones are firewood, scarce and limber.
The rain has frozen the creosote.

By winter the shells of their eyes will rive
nearer the hot coals. The sun
will seep from trees like milkweed.
The children will settle for the steam of the earth,
and for the chimneys to the North,
they will carry bales of chopped timber.

El Paso, 1983

VILLANELLE FOR VERONICA ARGUELLO (1975-1988)

She has been in time too short a light
we've fathered from the longest hour of day.
And cautiously the pain's tuneful turning we inherit.

And where the planted fields of rosewood and mesquite
allow the dark acacian root to shroud or fade,
she has been in time too short a light

to mother all the world's impermanence we hold inviolate,
and now her breath antiques a planet's motion, the way
words do, cautiously, their pain's tuneful turning we inherit.

Say to the Argentine river as it bends to find the prophet
moon, breathe still and be for the horizon the heartscape
she has been, in time too short a light

to know what age or altar bodies curse to spite
indifference. Commandante, for the missionary's sake, pray
for the cautious pain's tuneful turning we inherit.

What garland, what doll's dominion, what innocent slight
or refusal had she known or promised death to pay?
She has been in time too short a light
to know how cautiously the pain's tuneful turning we inherit.

THE LAKE ISLE OF BLED

I still see the bones of Bled through mirrors
and light the rock shade stores within its sepulcher,
how from the stoneyard eyes appear
like fish leaves nettled in spoors
of prehistoric clay. Across the rockfall
coins click down across their saintly feet
while from the gilded nave the wishbell
rings for the memory their minds will keep
long and unattended. All day I climb
with saurian soles to where the sun steam settles
and the hunched nun, blind on glacier lime,
blows the holy smoke from spears of candles.
She resents the circling swans that seine to rest.
She would rather see, and seeing, be the bones of death.

Yugoslavia, 1984

STANDING AT PASTERNAK'S TABLE

Birch bark, soundings in the linden wood,
ferns ornate as creweled cloth or filigree,
prints of birdscape in pastures and old sod—
These, like May light, he could not spare as easily
as I might, but memorized the Urals
in floats of geraniums unloamed from pots,
vowels of sunlight along the sill.
What the world had named, was neither poem nor art,
as if to walk in cadence were voiceless, doggerel
laced like shoes to slow his feet.
Words should grow inquisitive, become avowals,
as in birth or naming the unnamed, how brief
their passage of identity, yet precious
their fidelity to all nature's voice.

Peredelkino, 1985

33

A KILLING IN THE OLD COUNTRY

In her sack she feels the rope, thinks
how quick the spokes of the neck
will snap, tighter than the braid
wheat spins in the barn's souring chaff.
She knows the air is hay,
and seeds the chickens peck are fevered.

She walks hunched down along the trough,
the rib of light lasered by the rafter's coop.
All noon long, her shifting eyes
decide the course the earth will take
to shake the sun free. And what

she thinks will the difference make
if in the killing of a hen
this morning her lone child running
a pigling through the goldenrod,
finds the feathers sickled from the gilder's hair?

She knows the old country, the earth
will never move faster than the night stars,
and hearts she keeps
locked in the bone-bowl of her bed
will never beat in her crippling hands.

Her sudden eye is caught.
She feels for the noose and swift
as the half sign of the cross,
strangle-grips the cackler's craw,
the right hand not knowing the other,
cycling the knot, has shucked the whimper off.

Cernina, Czechoslovakia 1968

LA VICTIME OF THE POLICE CHIEF'S GUN
IN PROFILE

In the end the mind will fall intimately
and with it all the country
I imagine, will recite its singing
sentence at the center of his skull.
    So it be when it be
and the eternal spark he dawns
at the temple's rim
outlives the bevelling dot.
A crisp extinction follows.
    and the end if at the end
begins. A light, a ladder, nothing
will spiral through the head's implanted
leap of thought, not conclusion,
nor the altitude he hopes to climb
like shelves to a book long mastered.

Words will remain as solemn
as his eye, photographing everything
he will not see as permanent.
Not the air, not the angler's arm
in fish finder style, flailing the gravity
of lead's dead weight in space,
not the geysered spray of blood into
the right ear's foundling fire.
    He thinks if he thinks
he will not know the difference
future makes for the truck delivering
rice at the square's aperture,
nor that death in the surrounding

territory of his face is sprawled
wide as a locust sky.
  He will think what we think
that tied or clutched
behind his back in bather fashion
we cannot fail to see
the loop of hands failed at prayer.

What he cannot tell in the militant
smile awatch nearby, the whistling
rill of teeth, jawed rigid, undisguised,
is that he will live to be as human as he thinks
the world can stand. Perception
upon perception he will die.
  So it be and must it be
in the privacy of a death
we see the *mortis* of a muscle, stocking white,
in tantrum for the camera's eye,
as if by interruption of a moment's passion
we violate all of history
in images too sudden to witness or imagine.

Saigon, 1968

THE BATS OF THE DOWAGER EMPRESS

The sound a bat makes—"shou ... "
is the word the Chinese guide gives
for longevity. Bats are favored
by assassins in the Emperor's hall
of myths.
      On the tapestry
within the gold throne room
of the summer palace, bats
weave and romance
in the calligraphy of silk,
their eyes fixed
talonly on the Dowager.
      Before her throne
to each side, two mirrors,
ageless, the size of lotus pools
face a companion
pair of mirrors, reflecting
the glass back and all that moves
behind
      as history or past.
The Dowager can never speak
directly to the adorer's eye,
but glances sideways tickishly,
as if to refract the stillness
interrupted
      by the breath stall
      in a eunuch's foot
      or a Manchu smile,
or a bat,
valanced by its ribs
from the gilded canopy of yarn—
      suspended
in the demon pose of peace.

THE DEBRIS STONE

In all matter razed or demised,
one mote of stone or ash survives
as essence.

—CAO YU

All humanity in sleep
will breathe through the sudden
dislocation of rock from image,
the skid soil of a stone's erosion,
willowing down
in small crumbs from the table of sky,
and the spark's explosion
in a Tien An Men lamp will seem as stippled
twigs of light falling
sadly through our eyes.
We will weep through
what will cease in the stone's mind
to be
   and all
   the chined shells of atoms
   rushing to embrace
   a collapsing universe
   will collide.
Confessions
in our sanctuaries will be high.
And the zag lines drawn
by hordes of seismographs
we have stored like prophets in our cities
will be little more than nuisance
interruptions:
   the hang-drip of water
   in the sink stall,
   cracks on Arctic faults.

No one to witness the goddess tumbling
from the trinity of wires.
Above the rocksill and tattersall
of dust's divinity, a space
as silent as a city
will survive.
            In Beijing
where played the *Internationale*
in the soaring calm of June,
will tents no more
leech their skins to the pavement's thigh.
What will cease in the night's litter
to be
            will be haulage
            for the fires
            at Babaoshan.
And all the debris in China
will roll forth,
note by note in our mind's ensemble,
to where the burnt odor of rock
presides
            and the body ash
            beneath the Minzhu flame
            burls our imagination.
And nothing will cease to exist,
not the Great Wall's facade,
not the Sian skulls,
nor the whorling motes of dust,
aged all in proportion,
racking forth across the Gobi
like shoots of eucalyptus bees,
razing all the world to conscience,
raising
            as if to birth
            all the prayered flesh

the bald gods of profanity
bury in demise.
And thus will generations recall
how memory, in whose rivered essence
time's just power flows,
pricks deep,
                infinite
                and fossiled
as heat across a smoldering savannah,
as serpents roiling in a Shanghai shawl.

Womb-Weary

. . . how space quakes . . . wild
to be born for no one's sake
—STÉPHANE MALLARMÉ

THE EXPLORATION OF SPACE
FOR THE TWENTIETH CENTURY POET

To get into it properly,
he grows a tree
on the earlobe
and swings from it gently
through the inner ear
and apple-fall of its own darkness.

He tells himself at night in bed
when one lost and lingering word
curls spinelessly
along the ear's kingdom of the vague
like a mosquito itching for interpretation
that a snake preys within
the hollow sound of silence.

That through its forked tongue
as if to mime a kiss
he must hiss out the nuisance,
its poet's drum
roaring through all of conscience
like a leeching gnat or bully.

That for the sake of truth
he will hold his tongue, survive
its molting breath. And worm the apple
through the long fall and endless ground
of his imagination. He tells himself,
for Christ's sake,
the rumor of a serpent
was God's own dying
creation.

OUT OF CONTEXT

" . . . horrible and fascinating."
—DAN RATHER, CBS NEWS
ON THE CHALLENGER TRAGEDY

Horrible and fascinating the image
of parts puffed and splitting, slow-motion,
once we freeze
the frame and upper quadrant
of the rocket's right booster,
it is fascinating how
where the sphere of loss is most defined
a flash of light like the universe beginning
sparks all future
healing of the sun and sky,
and no one knows how long
or why the slow ascent so altered
the sudden end of course; it's too soon
to speculate on the fate
of lost beginnings.

Notice its awful aura to the prayer fall.
Notice its hopeful spire to the prayer full.
Watch the awful spire to the prayer fall
through future. It is horrible
yet fascinating how the lives fly apart
like spuds in arcs of light,
like hands to the blinking eye,
like blinds to the blinking weary,
like breath to the blinking blind
the moment beyond throttle,
we are live here, I repeat
no word yet

of survivors adequate enough to speak
of life's extremities.
It is fascinating

yet horrible, we apologize
for the delay the scale model
of our deeds necessitates
in so short and dark a space.
The accident developed here
beneath the wings in gaseous billions.
Imagine the matter of power so imminent.
Imagine the power of matter so small.
Imagine the power of death so small
a matter against the infinite of all,
how the truth
when seen in miniature
against such blue and awful sky,
just slightly altered, falls short
like Icarus, space-aged and trusting
in the false fathoms of illusion.
The sea is always still the bottom
of our failed important failures.

THE ASTRONAUT

No matter what hour of the day
the rocket roars in sleep,
testing space
like bodyfalls
to the earth's blue bed,
he wakes his children,
eyes like moons,
and points the sun's rise
off the cratered crib,
east to west, and watches
tails of stars fall
like toads
through memory's Black Hole,
their aureoles of light, brief
as passing conversations,
uncertain and apocryphal.

ONCE THE PREHISTORIC MAN

struck deaf by the preternatural
roar of birth,
had thought his body holes
were bottomless, without breath
or voice.

In sleep or passion
where his feet had walked,
the ear slept too, listening
among the lichens and spoors
for conversations of toads,

their slithering tails
falling through the body hole
of earth's black rock,
bottomless, without breath
or voice.

BREATH

*Our arms and legs are full
of sleeping memories of the past.*
—PROUST

1

Tugs the skin so hard in sleep
the limbs expand, as if
we could swing an arm out, width
and length-wise along the furniture
of a whole forest, and cull it in
across the vast moon of a field or planet
to our own small room.

In the high trees of imagination,
in our free breath, we tease ourselves
to crawl to the top of a pine, inhale
an aspen, stoke it in the sun,
its sweet aroma roiling in the fragile air,
and stepping down still
in the dark of our own sleep's bed, we study
the mind's way out.

2

At night in the ward-room practicing death,
my father, with owed breath tucked
in the bed of his lungs,
learned the punctual notes of leaving,
the dark that coal exhales
before the last grind of fire
whittles it to space. A railroad man

who toured the world-room in a Pullman,
he knew the blissful pass of the river for miles,
and would, when night burned out, stow
the moon's tall flame in ash.
In memory he owed the dark
each splice of rusted rail or sagging boxcar.
Breath, as in the sleep of legs,
he saved for the mind's departure.

TO THE BOILY BLIND BOY THE SUN SPINS

In his firmament
of body bones and braille,
when all else in the universe
collides or fails,
he will convince you
that the sun has water
in the green marrow of a stone,
that it spins
through space, freely
gathering speed, micro-slow,
warmed by the swash
of its own smoked sea.

He will argue that
seasons are illusions,
that the sun has never known
the cold dark of the galaxy,
the quick melt of a breeze
on a blanched rock.
In its rivers rainbows run
and whales arc like skeet
across the skyline.

He will convince you
of a planet in the fire's womb,
that there are hanging drills
and dinosaurs in heat,
that our future bears resemblance
to a slug or lunar weed,

that the Earth we breathe
is nothing

but the sun's dead moon passing,
icy wraith, sparked out,
a snake
spooled by a gunshot,
dust-sudden.

WAKING TO TWO MOONS

In our last century of sky,
a thin wind will sickle
the moon's truss of craters,
and two moons will spin
like peach halves into the universe.

Should your single eye
scale the precipice of space
to see how barren the language
of stars can be, how sullenly
the night ignores the passing
shell of one, fallow in its tow,
yet divines the other
in some fit of passion
it cannot check, you will know

the God-breath of stones, split
in the twin pose of infinity,
how the sky in love is humbled
by the intimacy of birth.

And sleeping to two moons,
sheep will praise the cloved wheat;
hedgehogs will raise the hamper husks
of snouts to outreach light;
cattle lull the haunch of rumps
they waddle and brisk deliriously
through a green stream at dawn.

When you awake and go on
dreaming everything as one and round,
what you will find

is only a peach half
left behind on a bed dish,
and the true moon balloons
in the eye of a woman you will love
in any ocean or crater of dust.

THE MIND IMAGINED (THE HEART IMAGINED)

After a long time away the mind imagined
   daughter screws on the tossed
   bald belly of a Chinese doll
   she has sprayed with crayon grist
   to keep its memory alive.

After a long time away the mind imagined
   son sleeps on sheets of cut glass,
   and the trellised ribs of pavement
   warm the homeboy growing slow
   to fetch a dime of concrete conversation.

After a long time away the mind imagined
   beds of gaytown, sadtown,
   and the alltown dead,
   hanging in bleak rivers of light,
   dry their bones on winter birch
   in the darkest forest of day.

After a long time away the imagined minds
   the sill of fences in Soweto
   where the guard dogs rise
   like suns in the eyes of infants,
   and where on rooftops, thatched and flaming,
   sods of flesh fan the winds of Kalihari.

After a long time away the mind imagines
   the humane apathia, the divine
   euthanasia for rivers unknown,
   whetting the raintree's frozen marrow
   on the earth's abode of stones.

After a long time away the mind imagines
   a city with no soundings
   the pettish might tune for language,
   a country of syllables, still as Beckett breath,
   in whose carapace of thought
   words like ill neighborings lodge,
   mute as grisling in a can.

After a long time away the heart imagines
   a universe, turned backwards on its back,
   a chain of stars tied to its waist,
   and in such space as this the imagined
   mind, face down, and breathing
   barely, snorts a short distance away.

A BOY FALLS INTO SPACE AT THE STONE QUARRY

a.

Where in the boy is the mind still listening
to wind-splash the linnets maw to barking brants
among the swales and willows of highland clay?

Where is the rook he goggled and the noon cows
drovers swished along with shoots of jonquil bells
down the cliffside to middling and hobo caves?

Nowhere have his feet borne the welts of sabots
trussed in jagger thorns and lace the father mapped
with drove and hammer to suit familiar ground.

Nowhere are his brawned lobes of fingers touching
lips so galed the mother smiles. Nowhere is sleep
so sudden as dark cradling in a child's caul.

b.

He has found the world too much for lingering
interpretations or decisions the mind's
weather makes to keep imagination free.

In his youth he might have wondered why in spite
of all deep emotion, God-leaves were falling
and the bed he made had spermed from the earth's spring

shallows like stones. Still, enough has been enough
of all the bride-grooming reason gives the heart.
He has heard the body's deep bone rattle once

too often, the heart's heart breathing through the quick
blood, pumping him of all thought or experience.
He is at rest now, womb-weary and travelled.

Born in Duquesne, Pa., **James Ragan** received his B.A. at St. Vincent College and his M.A. and Ph.D. at Ohio University. He has lived in Czechoslovakia, Paris, Athens, and Beijing and has been honored here and abroad as an ambassador of poetry. In 1985 he was one of three Americans, including Robert Bly and Bob Dylan, invited to perform at the First International Poetry Festival in Moscow. In 1988, he performed in China at the invitation of the Beijing Writers Union. Again, in 1990 he performed for the U.S. Ambassador in Moscow. Other venues have included Tokyo, Hong Kong, London, Sofia, Paris and Prague. James Ragan is the recipient of numerous poetry honors, including two Fulbright Professorships (Yugoslavia and China), the Emerson Poetry Prize, two Pushcart Prize nominations, and a Poetry Society of America Gertrude Claytor Award. He is the author of **In the Talking Hours** and the plays *Saints* and *commedia* (first produced by Raymond Burr in the U.S. and later in the Soviet Union). The co-editor of the **Collected Poems of Yevgeny Yevtushenko,** he is the Director of the Graduate Professional Writing Program at the University of Southern California.